# Land of Eternal Spring
## Wonderfully Exotic Recipes of Guatemala

# Tierra de Primavera Eterna
## Recetas Maravillosas y Exóticas de Guatemala

**Mark Gargus**

ISBN 978-1519690852

# Welcome to the Mayan World
# Bienvenidos al Mundo Maya

It was not long ago finding a "Real" Mexican restaurant was impossible unless you lived in the southwest near the Mexican border or a very large metropolis. Trying to make the food at home was equally daunting as the needed ingredients were nearly impossible to find. In the ensuing years, many Latin/Mexican restaurants have sprung up. Though to this day, few are authentic – the same can be said for many Asian offerings. Thankfully, the grocery scene has improved tremendously. Tiendas have appeared in nearly every community and often the larger supermarkets have an extensive selection of Latin essentials.

Currently, finding an authentic Guatemalan restaurant is unlikely. Fortunately the  availability of ingredients makes preparing Guatemalan food at home possible – if you have the recipes.

This book is one of the few available in English. For those who speak some Spanish, Guatemalan recipes can still be confusing. Many ingredients are unique to Central America, though there are substitutes that are nearly the same. Also, a number of other ingredients change their names when crossing the border from Mexico to Central America – a few examples – Chayote = Güisquil, Chiles Anchos = Chiles Pasas. I have always been an avid cook, including Mexican cuisine. Being from the US and after having lived in Guatemala for seven years, I have been able to determine good substitutions and resolve the nomenclature issues.

One would assume Guatemalan and Mexican cuisines would be very similar given their proximity. With the exception of a few Mexican dishes from Yucatan and Chiapas, this is not the case. Guatemalan cuisine has a strong Mayan influence versus the Aztec – Toltec influence in Mexican favorites. Guatemalan food is noted for rich, savory sauces with a spicy sauce such as Chirmól served on the side. Many of the recipes in this book are authentic Mayan. Other recipes reflect the blending of European and indigenous cultures over the centuries.

# Contents

# Appetizers - Botanas

## Anacate Mushrooms Provençal Style – Anacates Provençal

Anacates are wild mushrooms which grow in the cloud forests of Guatemala. Any sort of full flavored mushrooms can be substituted – crimini (baby bella), fresh shitakes, etc.

Coarsely grate
> ¼ cup mozzarella

Mince
> 2 medium cloves garlic

Thickly slice
> 1½ lbs mushrooms

In a large skillet sauté for 1-2 minutes – don't burn the garlic
> ¼ cup olive oil
> Minced garlic

Add the mushrooms and cook covered over medium heat for 3 minutes, tossing a few times. Add and cook uncovered over low heat for 4 minutes, tossing a few times.
> 1½ tsp basil
> 1½ tsp rosemary (finely chopped or ground)
> ½ tsp marjoram
> ½ tsp oregano
> ½ tsp thyme
> 1 tsp salt

Add, cover and cook slowly for 5 minutes, tossing a few times
> ½ cup dry white wine

Prepare a serving plate by covering with a bed of
> Lettuce leaves

Just before serving, add and cook uncovered over low heat for 4 minutes, tossing a few times.
> 1½ Tbsp lime or lemon juice
> 2 tsp Tabasco

Place on the lettuce leaves and sprinkle with
> Grated mozzarella

## Baked Pumpkin Pies – Empanadas de Ayote

These savory Guatemalan empanadas most closely resemble fried pies in the US, though these are baked rather than fried.

This recipe calls for pumpkin purée.

 2

Sometimes it available canned. Sometimes canned 100% pumpkin is available – simply purée in a food processor. Canned pumpkin pie filling is not a suitable substitute. To make it with fresh pumpkin, in a steamer cook for about 50 minutes

> 1 small pumpkin, seeded and quartered

When it is fork tender, allow to cool somewhat, scrape off the flesh and purée. If this is more than you need, the excess may be frozen.

To make the dough – the procedure is very similar to pie crust, basic rule – do not overmix

> In a large bowl, combine
>
>> 2 cups flour
>>
>> 1 tsp salt
>
> Cut in
>
>> ⅔ cup shortening
>
> Combine
>
>> ¼ cup water
>>
>> 1 Tbsp hot sauce like Tabasco
>
> Slowly combine the liquid with the flour mixture with a fork, taking care not to overmix. Cover and refrigerate for at least an hour.

For the filling

> Cover with boiling water, allow to sit for 10 minutes and drain
>
>> 2 Tbsp raisins
>
> In a large skillet, heat
>
>> 2 Tbsp oil
>
> Add and cook until transparent
>
>> 1 medium chopped onion
>
> Add and cook until the beef is browned, smashing the meat with a spoon occasionally to break up large chunks
>
>> ¼ lb very lean ground beef
>>
>> 1 clove finely chopped garlic
>>
>> 1 tsp cayenne pepper
>>
>> 1 tsp salt
>>
>> ½ tsp ground cumin
>>
>> ½ tsp ground cinnamon
>
> Allow to cool some, add and mix well
>
>> 1 cup pumpkin puree

Preheat oven to 370°F

3

Divide the dough into 8 pieces. On a well floured board, roll out each piece to 5″-6″ in diameter. Place ⅛ of the filling in the center of each empananda. Dampen the edges with water, fold over and seal well. Place on a non-stick baking sheet and brush with

  1 lightly beaten egg

Bake in preheated oven for 20-30 minutes until lightly browned

## Cheese Ceviche – Ceviche de Queso Panela

Panela cheese can be found in some Latin groceries. The most common brand in the US is Cacique. If unavailable, a flavorful mozzarella can be substituted.

Cut into ½″ cubes and place in a bowl

  ½ lb panela cheese

Finely chop and add to the cheese

  ½ lb husked tomatillos (miltomates)

  2 large sprigs cilantro

  1 small red onion

  1 large stalk celery

Add and refrigerate for at least 30 minutes

  ¼ cup lime juice

  1 Tbsp Worcestershire sauce

  1 Tbsp ground toasted pumpkin seeds (optional)

  1 Tbsp olive oil

  1½ tsp salt – or to taste

Before serving, dice

  1 avocado

Serve, garnishing with diced avocado

## Guatemalan Enchiladas – Enchiladas Chapín

Anyone who has experienced Mexican enchiladas is in for a surprise. We have also included a recipe for the Mexican version in the poultry section as our Guatemalan neighbors thought they were excellent.

Have on hand

  1 bag 3″-4″ round tostadas – those sold in Latin groceries are more authentic and less salty

Top each tostada with

  Finely chopped cooked beets

  or

  Refried beans

Sprinkle with

4

Crumbled queso fresco

## Guatemalan Guacamole – Guacamól Chapín

Smoother texture and seasoned differently than the Mexican version

Purée
>	Flesh from 4 avocados

Finely chop
>	1 medium onion

Mix the avocados and onion with
>	1 cup lime juice
>	½ tsp oregano
>	Salt to taste
>	1 tsp Tabasco or to taste

Garnish with
>	Finely chopped cilantro

## Guatemalan Marinated Seafood – Ceviche Chapín

Guatemalan ceviche is much more strongly seasoned than its Mexican counterpart. Many Guatemalans prefer the Mexican version, so its recipe follows.

Parboil for 5 minutes
>	1 lb fillets from very fresh, firm fleshed fish, shellfish or assortment cut into ½" cubes

Drain, add and marinate for ½ hour
>	Juice from 3 limes
>	2 Tbsp Worcestershire

Roughly chop
>	5 Roma tomatoes

Finely chop
>	1 medium onion
>	5-6 large sprigs cilantro
>	2-3 sprigs mint
>	1 clove garlic

Add the chopped ingredients to the marinating seafood along with
>	½ tsp pepper
>	½ tsp salt or to taste
>	½ tsp Tabasco

Ceviche is typically served with saltine crackers and in some places, hot tortillas.

## Mexican Guacamole – Guacamól Mexicano

Broil or roast until mostly blackened on all sides

    1-2 chiles serranos

Place in a plastic bag for about 10 minutes, rinse off most of the black and de-seed

Pulse until almost smooth in a food processor

    ¼ small onion, finely chopped

    2 cloves garlic

    Serranos

    2-4 sprigs cilantro

    ¼ tsp salt

    Flesh from one avocado

    Juice of one lime

Add and pulse a few times, leaving some texture

    Flesh from 2 avocados

    1 large tomato – peeled using the boiling method, seeded and chopped

    ¼ small onion, coarsely chopped

    2-4 sprigs cilantro

## Mexican Marinated Seafood – Ceviche Mexicano

Place in boiling water for 10-15 seconds

    1 medium tomato

While hot, remove skin, seed and chop

Cut into ½" cubes

    ½ lb fillets from very fresh, firm fleshed fish or shellfish

Combine and refrigerate for 4 hours

    Cubes of fish

    Juice of 3 large limes

    Chopped tomato

    2 Tbsp olive oil

    ¼ tsp oregano

    ¼ tsp salt

    ½ tsp pepper

Before serving garnish with

    1 Tbsp chopped cilantro

    Thin slices of onion and/or avocado

Ceviche is typically served with saltine crackers

## Quesadillas with Rosa de Jamaica – Quesadillas con Rosa de Jamaica

Rosa de Jamaica (pronounced ha-my-ka) is a type of dried hibiscus, commonly used to make a tea or if the tea is strong, a mixer for cocktails. It is commonly found in Latin groceries in half pound bags. After making the tea, the flowers are usually discarded, but in this recipe they are used as a flavoring ingredient.

In a small saucepan, bring to a boíl, reduce to a simmer and cook for 10-15 minutes until the flowers are al dente

> ½ cup Rosa de Jamaica
> Enough water to cover by 1″

Drain the flowers and allow to cool, reserving the liquid for some tea or cocktails

Coarsely grate

> 1½ cups flavorful hard or semi-hard cheese

Sauté a few minutes, until onions are translucent

> 2 Tbsp olive oil
> 1 small diced onion

Add and sauté about 4 minutes more

> Coarsely chopped Rosa de Jamaica
> ¼ tsp salt

Using

> 8 corn tortillas

Prepare each quesadilla as follows. On one tortilla, add about ⅛ of the cheese, ¼ of the Rosa de Jamaica mixture and another ⅛ of the cheese. Top with another tortilla. Repeat with the remaining ingredients.

When ready to cook, preheat oven to 200°F

Heat a large skillet or griddle over medium high heat. Heat as many quesadillas as will fit in your skillet, for 3-4 minutes per side. Mash down gently to assist everything sticking together. Place in warm oven until ready to serve.


## Salpicón

Though the end result looks as though it was made with regular ground beef – it is made with cooked meat, subsequently finely chopped.

Cook until medium rare or well done, depending on your preference

> 1 lb eye of round
> 1 medium onion, quartered
> 1 tsp salt

Allow the meat to cool and chop finely or pulse ½″ cubes in a food processor until it resembles coarsely ground hamburger.

Finely chop
  1 medium onion
  4 large sprigs mint
Mix the beef and chopped onion and mint with
  ¼ cup lime juice
  Salt to taste

## Shrimp Ceviche  with Chilies and Radishes – Ceviche de Camarones con Chiles y Rábanos

In a medium bowl combine
  1 lb peeled and cleaned shrimp
  ¾ cup fresh lime juice
  2 jalapeño or serrano chilies, finely sliced – optionally remove seeds for less heat
  ¼ cup finely sliced red onion
  1 Tbsp salt
  1 Tbsp olive oil
Cover and refrigerate. After 2 hours add
  ½ lb chopped radishes
  ½ cup chopped tomatoes
  ¼ cup chopped cilantro
Cover and refrigerate 2 hours more. Serve with saltine crackers.

# Sauces, Seasonings and Stuffings
## Salsas, Sazones y Rellenos

 9

## Green Tomatillo Sauce – Salsa de Miltomates

Broil or roast until mostly blackened on all sides
> 1-2 chiles serranos

Place in a plastic bag for about 10 minutes, rinse off most of the black and de-seed
Prepare by removing husks, placing in boiling water and simmering for 10 minutes
> ½ lb husked tomatillos (miltomates)

Pulse until almost smooth in a food processor
> Serranos
> ¼ small onion
> 1 clove garlic
> 2 large sprigs cilantro
> 2 Tbsp water
> ¼ tsp salt
> 1 or 2 of the tomatillos

Add and pulse, leaving some texture
> The remaining tomatillos
> Pinch of sugar

## Guatemalan Cooked Tomato Sauce – Chirmól Chapín

Similar to Salsa Ranchera but seasoned a bit differently. In addition to huevos rancheros is also excellent on grilled meats. It may be served hot or at room temperature.

Broil, turning as needed to blacken on all sides
> 8-10 Roma tomatoes

Finely chop
> 1 small onion
> 1 large sprig cilantro

Coarsely chop
> Broiled tomatoes

Combine
> Chopped ingredients
> Juice from 1 lime
> 1 tsp pepper
> ½ tsp salt or to taste
> 1 tsp Tabasco

Portions may be frozen

## Guatemalan Pico de Gallo – Chirmól

Chirmól is Guatemala's version of Mexican Pico de Gallo and is sometimes called Pico de Gallo. Though most Guatemalan food is milder than similar Mexican counterparts, this is an exception.

Macerate with a mortar and pestle

>1oz chiltepes (or 2-3 jalapeños or serranos)

Combine chilis with

>2 finely chopped medium tomatoes, including juice
>
>1 finely chopped medium white onion
>
>Juice from one large lime
>
>Salt to taste

Allow at least 1 hour for the flavors to come together

## Ranch Style Tomato Sauce – Salsa Ranchera

Broil or roast until mostly blackened on all sides

>3 chiles serranos or 1-2 jalapeños

Place in a plastic bag for about 10 minutes, rinse off most of the black and de-seed

Broil until lightly blackened

>1 medium tomato

Finely chop in a food processor

>Chiles
>
>1 large clove garlic

Add a pulse a few times to coarsely chop

>Tomato

In a skillet sauté until tender but not brown

>1 Tbsp oil
>
>1 small finely chopped onion

Add and sauté about 5 minutes, until somewhat thickened.

>Pureed ingredients
>
>¼ tsp salt

## Sazón

Several brands are available in Latin groceries but most contain MSG. Here is a more natural version.

    1 Tbsp ground coriander
    1 Tbsp ground cumin
    1 Tbsp ground annatto seeds (achiote)
    1 Tbsp garlic powder
    1 Tbsp salt
    2 tsp oregano
    1 tsp ground black pepper

## Turkey Stuffing – Relleno para Pavo

Tired of sage or oyster dressing for your turkey? Here's a Guatemalan alternative sufficient for a 14 lb bird.
In a small skillet sauté until browned

    1 lb ground pork
    1 Tbsp oil if the pork is very lean
    ½ tsp salt
    1 tsp pepper

In a large skillet sauté

    1 Tbsp oil
    ½ lb thinly sliced green beans
    ½ lb peeled and diced carrots
    1 large clove minced garlic
    2-3 bay leaves

After a few minutes, add and continue to sauté

    ½ lb diced potatoes

When the potatoes are slightly tender, add the previously browned pork and mix well. If the resulting mixture seems dry, add

    ½ - 1 cup chicken stock

# Salads - Ensaladas

## Cold Plate for Day of the Dead – Fiambre Tradicional

A very Guatemalan tradition. Typically prepared for Day of the Dead (October 31) and All Saints Day (November 1) and most frequently consumed in the cemetery at the graves of dear departed relatives. Every family's combination is somewhat different and can vary from year to year. Some fiambres contain 50 or so different items.  As such, only general guidelines are presented here.

On a large platter, on a bed of lettuce, artfully arrange an assortment of
> Cured meats and sausages
> Sliced cheeses
> Pickled, canned and steamed fresh vegetables – to be really authentic, be sure to include beets
> Sliced hardboiled eggs
> Sliced radishes

Whatever you do, you can claim yours is the best. Everyone in Guatemala does.

## Fresh Pimento Salad – Ensalada de Chiles Pimientos

Broil or roast until mostly blackened on all sides
> 1 large red bell pepper

Place in a plastic bag for about 10 minutes, rinse off most of the black and de-seed
Slice the red peppers into thin strips and combine with
> 2 finely chopped cloves of garlic
> 1½ Tbsp olive oil
> 1 Tbsp red wine vinegar
> ¼ tsp salt

Allow to marinate at least 1 hour (or better yet, overnight in the refrigerator) before serving. This heavenly salad is excellent served with grilled meats.

## Fried Pork Rind Salad – Chojin

The principal ingredient in this recipe is fried pork rinds. Try to find them in a Latin grocery – the prepackaged varieties tend to lack authenticity.

This recipe calls for hot (warm) fried pork rinds – if those you can find are room temperature, place in a preheated oven for 5-10 minutes
> ½ lb fried pork rinds

Grate
> 4oz queso seco (Romano can be substituted)

Combine
> ¼ lb finely chopped radishes
> 1 medium onion, finely chopped

14

2-3 Roma tomatoes

Juice of 2-4 limes – depending on size

2 Tbsp chopped parsley

1-2 finely chopped Serrano peppers

Hot pork rinds

Before serving sprinkle with grated cheese

## Lightly Pickled Salad – Ensalada en Escabeche

Parboil until barely tender, all or an assortment of

5 carrots, peeled and sliced (not too finely)

1 cauliflower, cut into florets

1 broccoli, cut into florets

1 lb green beans, ends snapped off and cut into 2-3 pieces

1 lb peas (if using frozen peas, add near the end of the cooking process)

2-3 chopped jalapenos (optional, but escabeche is typically a bit hot)

Several large sliced radishes

Enough water to cover

1 tsp salt

Drain and allow to cool

In a large skillet, sauté until tender

1 lb coarsely chopped onion

5-10 (depending on size and taste) coarsely chopped cloves garlic

5 coarsely chopped bell peppers

When tender place in a large pot with the parboiled vegetables, add and bring to a boil

½ cup vinegar

Enough water to barely cover

1-2 tsp salt

1 tsp thyme

3 bay leaves

A few minutes after bringing to a boil, taste for vinegar and salt. Caution - this dish is served cold and the flavor of salt intensifies when cooled. Chill and serve within a few days.

## Tomato Salad with Cheese, Olives, and Mint – Ensalada de Tomate, Queso, Olivas y Menta

The original version of this recipe calls for cotija cheese – feta is very similar in taste and texture and may be substituted.

Cut out stem end, thickly slice and place in a salad serving bowl

     2 lb tomatoes

Add and toss lightly

     2 Tbsp olive oil

     ¼ tsp salt

     ½ tsp pepper

Place over top

     ¼ cup cotija cheese

     2 Tbsp minced mint

     ½ cup sliced black olives

# Eggs and Cheese
# Huevos y Queso

## Cheese Turnovers – Dobladas de Queso en Mantequilla

Sort of a Latin grilled cheese sandwich. A cholesterol laden delight! This recipe calls for queso de capas. It is a firm, not crumbly version of queso fresco. Mozzarella or other mild, semi firm cheese can be substituted.
Slice, about the size of half a tortilla
> 9 pieces queso de capas

Place the cheese on and fold over
> 9 corn tortillas

In a large skillet, heat until bubbling and reduce heat
> 3 Tbsp butter

Fry the cheese filled tortillas about 30 seconds per side – you may need to do this in batches and add more butter if needed. To the remaining butter, whisk in
> ¼ cup heavy cream or crema

Pour over tortillas before serving


## Eggs Poached in Tomato Broth – Huevos Escalfados en Caldo de Tomate

Serve with plenty of hot tortillas and maybe some refried beans on the side. Recipe can easily be doubled, just use a larger saucepan or pot.
Char, peel and cut into ⅛" strips
> 3 – 4 poblano chilies

Slice into 6 wedges, about ⅜" thick
> 4 – 6oz queso fresco

Broil until lightly charred on all sides
> 1 lb of ripe fresh tomatoes

Blend the tomatoes for a few seconds, leaving some texture
In a saucepan large enough in diameter to accommodate the poaching eggs, sauté until translucent
> 2 Tbsp oil
> ¾ cup thinly sliced onion

Add and cook about 3 more minutes
> The chili strips

Add the blended tomatoes and cook over fairly high heat for 6 – 10 minutes until somewhat reduced. Add and bring to boil
> 1½ cups water
> Salt to taste

Reduce to simmer. Break one by one into a saucer and gently slide into the simmering tomato broth.
> 6 eggs

Place a piece of queso fresco on top of each egg. Cover saucepan and poach eggs slowly for 6 – 8 minutes.

18

## Guatemalan Omelets – Tortilla de Huevo

When one says omelet to Guatemalans, it is usually met with a puzzled look. This recipe is basically an omelet, with similar, but often different fillings.

Prepare one of the following fillings adjusting quantities for the size of the omelet

Savory fillings

> Sautéed mushrooms and onions, seasoned with fresh herbs and grated cheese
>
> Thin slices of avocado, tomato and bell pepper, thinly sliced roast beef, mixed with a little crema
>
> Diced cooked pork or chicken with grated cheese, mixed with a little crema
>
> When ready to serve top any of the above with any or all of
>
> > Chopped parsley
> >
> > Thinly sliced bell pepper
> >
> > Thinly sliced avocado
> >
> > Crumbled crispy fried bacon

Sweet fillings

> Lightly toasted nuts and/or chopped strawberries, raspberries or blackberries combined with beaten, sweetened whipping cream.
>
> When ready to serve sprinkle with
>
> > Powdered sugar

Beat as you would for an omelet – quantities are for 2 eggs – 1 serving

> 2 eggs
>
> 2 tsp beer
>
> ¼ tsp pepper (omit for sweet versions)
>
> ¼ tsp salt (omit for sweet versions)
>
> ¼ tsp Tabasco (omit for sweet versions)

Heat in a medium to large skillet (depending on the quantity of eggs)

> 1½ -3 Tbsp butter

When the bubbles begin to subside, add the beaten eggs. Reduce heat and cook until almost set, lifting the edges from time to time, distributing the uncooked egg to the edges. Place the filling on one half of the omelet and cook a few minutes more over low heat. Flip the unfilled side over the filled side a cook a minute or two more. Top with savory or sweet toppings and serve.

## Ranch Style Eggs – Huevos a la Ranchera

This dish is typically made with fried (sunny side up) eggs, though can be made with scrambled eggs or omelets. Note to visitors – when ordering breakfast, you will be automatically served sauce with fried eggs (huevos fritos). If you prefer another style of egg, alert your server that you want some Ranchera sauce and they will gladly bring you some.

Prepare a batch of Salsa Ranchera or Chirmol

Fry sunny side up, firm to runny, depending on your preference

    8 eggs

Cover with salsa and serve with hot tortillas, refried beans and fried plantains.

## Scrambled Eggs with Tomato and Onion – Huevos Revueltos con Tomate y Cebolla

Finely chop

    ¼ cup onion

    ¼ cup ripe seeded tomato

Beat well

    4 eggs

Add the chopped vegetables

Scramble in a medium lightly oiled skillet until somewhat dry.

Serve with hot sauce, tortillas, refried beans and maybe some fried plantains.

# Starches and Beans
# Almidones y Frijoles

## Banana Leaves Stuffed with Potato and Meat – Paches

Sort of a tamale made with something other than corn masa. Sometimes made with rice sometimes made with potatoes, this recipe is made with potatoes. Generally more highly seasoned than tamales. At Christmastime, every household makes their own version. Other times of the year, tiendas make paches on Saturday evenings. To display the availability, they hang red lanterns. This causes some confusion among people from most other countries where red lanterns signify something altogether different.

Freshly made, yellowish lard is very common in the mercados of Guatemala – it is much more flavorful than the white refined product that can sometimes be found elsewhere. The best substitute is vegetable shortening.

Bring some water to a boil in a small saucepan, turn off heat, add and allow to cook for about 10 minutes

> ½ lb husked tomatillos (miltomates)

Drain and set aside

Boil until done

> 1½ lb pork, such as Boston butt – chicken is often substituted, about 2 lb legs and thighs
> 1 tsp salt
> Plenty of water to cover

Remove the pork and cook in the same water until tender

> 6 lb peeled potatoes
> 2 diced bell peppers
> 2 cloves minced garlic

While the potatoes and vegetables are cooking, shred cooked pork into small pieces – if chicken, debone and shred

When the potatoes and vegetables are done, mash as you would for mashed potatoes along with

> Drained tomatillos
> 2 tsp allspice
> 1 tsp pepper
> 1 tsp ground annatto (achiote)
> 1 tsp cayenne
> ½ lb lard

Most commonly paches are wrapped in machán leaves, though banana or plantain leaves would work well, too. The following assembly instructions assume you can find any of the above. If not, check out one of the recipes for tamales using corn husks for assembly – the end result will be about the same.

Pass over heat to soften a bit – gas burners work the best.

> A large leaf

Cut into approximately 8"x8" squares. Place about ¼ cup of the potato mixture in the center and add several strips of meat. Fold the edges over to make approximately 2½ x 5" packages. Loosely tie with cotton kitchen twine – in Guatemala there is a vegetable fiber called cibaque, but probably impossible to find elsewhere. Repeat with the remaining ingredients.

Place the assembled paches in a large steamer. Steam for about 40 minutes.

## Fried Black Beans – Frijolitos Fritos

A way to kick up canned black beans. Typically served on top of tostadas (the Latin brands are less salty) with some crumbled queso fresco (available in Latin groceries or in supermarkets with a decent Latin section)

Finely chop
> 1 large onion

Coarsely chop
> 2-3 tomatoes

Heat in a large skillet
> 2 Tbsp oil

Sauté until tender
> Chopped onion

Add the chopped tomato and cook a few minutes. Add and cook for 5-10 minutes until fork tender
> 1 can (approx 20oz) whole black beans (La Costeña and Ducal are common brands)

Serve as described above

## Green Rice – Arróz Verde

Cover with hot water for about 5 minutes
> 1½ cups long grain rice

Strain, rinse well and allow to drain

In a blender puree
> 1 small bunch parsley
> 4 large sprigs cilantro
> 3 – 4 romaine lettuce leaves
> 2 small or 1 large poblano chilies, seeded and roughly chopped (do not char or peel)
> ½ small onion chopped
> 1 clove of garlic
> ½ cup water

You will probably need to turn the blender off a few times and mash the ingredients down

In a large saucepan, heat over high heat
> ¼ cup oil

Add and stir frequently for up to 10 minutes or until rice is a pale gold color.

> Strained rice

Pour or blot out excess oil

Add and cook on high heat for about 3 minutes or until somewhat dry

> Green puree

Add, stir well once, and cook over medium heat until the liquid is absorbed and bubbles form on the top of the rice – about 10 minutes

> 3 cups hot salty chicken stock

Cover, reduce heat to low and cook 5 more minutes.

Remove from heat and set aside covered for about 20 minutes.


## Piloyes Antigua Style – Piloyada Antigüeña

Red beans in Guatemala generally are small and resemble adzuki beans. However, piloyes are very similar to kidney beans. A common brand in the US is Camellia, used for making the classic New Orleans red beans and rice. Many Guatemalans use more or different types of sausages and meats – substitute to your heart's content.

The day before, combine and allow to soak

> ½ lb piloyes
>
> 3 cups water

The next day, cook the beans in the soaking water until tender. Drain, reserving 1 cup of the cooking liquid

NOTE: As a time saving measure, you could probably use 2 16oz cans drained kidney beans, reserving 1 cup of the liquid.

In either case, combine the drained beans with enough water to cover and

> 2 Tbsp vinegar

Allow to marinate for about 6 hours and drain.

While the beans are marinating

Combine and simmer until the chicken is done

> 1 chicken breast
>
> ½ tsp salt
>
> Enough water to cover

Roughly chop the chicken and reduce the cooking liquid to ½ cup

In a skillet, cook

> 4 longaniza sausages – or other type of chorizo – stabbed with a sharp fork to help the grease escape
>
> ¼ cup water

24

When nicely browned, remove and slice into ¼″ rounds
Finely chop
>       2 Tbsp parsley
>       1 medium onion
Coarsely chop
>       ½ lb tomatoes
>       1 green bell pepper
Grate
>       2 Tbsp queso seco (Romano is a good substitute)
Optionally, prepare
>       1 hardboiled egg
Drain the marinated beans and add
>       1 cup reserved bean liquid
>       Chopped vegetables
>       4 bay leaves
>       1 tsp thyme
Mix well and add to the beans and vegetables
>       2 Tbsp vinegar
>       2 Tbsp olive oil
Sprinkle with the grated cheese and optionally garnish with
>       Sliced hardboiled egg

## Red Beans with Fresh Thyme – Piloyes con Tomillo Fresco

Red beans in Guatemala generally are small and resemble adzuki beans. However, piloyes are very similar to kidney beans. A common brand in the US is Camellia, used for making the classic New Orleans red beans and rice.

The day before, combine and allow to soak
>       ½ lb piloyes
>       3 cups water

NOTE: As a time saving measure, you could probably use 2 16oz cans drained kidney beans – cooking time will also be reduced.

In a large heavy pot, slowly cook until crispy
>       1 Tbsp olive oil
>       4 strips bacon

Remove and crumble bacon. In the same pot sauté until tender
>       1 cup diced carrot

Add to the pot, bring to a boil and reduce to a simmer for 45 minutes to 1½ hours until the beans are quite tender

 Crumbled bacon
 2 cloves minced garlic
 Drained beans
 2 large sprigs fresh thyme
 Enough water to cover by an inch or so

You may need to add more hot water to keep the beans covered. When the beans are tender, add salt to taste. Before serving, stir in

 1 Tbsp chopped fresh thyme leaves

Serve with crusty bread or over rice or polenta.

## Red Rice – Arróz Rojo

Cover with hot water for about 5 minutes

 1½ cups long grain rice

Strain, rinse well and allow to drain
In a blender puree

 1 lb fresh very ripe tomatoes (do not skin or seed) or 1 15oz can of tomatoes, drained
 1 small onion chopped
 1 clove of garlic

In a large saucepan, heat over high heat

 ¼ cup oil

Add and stir frequently for up to 10 minutes or until rice is a pale gold color.

 Strained rice

Pour or blot out excess oil
Add and cook on high heat for about 3 minutes or until somewhat dry

 Tomato puree

Add, stir well once, cover and cook over medium heat until the liquid is absorbed and bubbles form on the top of the rice – about 10 minutes

 3½ cups hot salty chicken stock
 ¼ cup fresh or frozen English peas (optional)
 1 small thinly sliced carrot (optional)
 1 large sprig parsley (optional)

Remove from heat and set aside covered for about 20 minutes.

## Rice with Chicken Broth – Arróz Hecho con Consomé de Pollo

Cover with hot water for about 5 minutes

> 1½ cups long grain rice

Strain, rinse well and drain

In a large saucepan, heat over high heat

> ¼ cup oil

Add and stir frequently for a few minutes until the rice is just turning color

> Strained rice

Add and continue to fry over high heat, until rice is pale golden and the onions are tender – the entire process should take less than 10 minutes

> 1 small onion finely chopped
> 1 clove minced or pressed garlic

Pour or blot out excess oil

Add, stir well once, and cook over medium heat until the liquid is absorbed and bubbles form on the top of the rice – about 10 minutes

> 3½ cups hot salty chicken stock
> Several sprigs parsley
> 1 small bay leaf
> ¼ tsp thyme

Remove from heat and set aside covered for about 20 minutes. Remove the bay leaf and parsley before serving.

## Small Plain Corn Tamales – Tamalitos

Plain tamalitos are as ubiquitous as bread in European culture or rice in Asian culture. They are served alongside practically everything, especially dishes of Mayan origin.

Makes 8 – 10, recipe can be easily increased

Combine and mix well with hands to make a rather stiff dough

> 2 cups masa harina (Maseca is a common brand available in the US)
> 1¼ cups warm water

Soak in warm water

> Enough dried corn husks for the number of tamalitos you plan to make (1-2 each, depending on the size of the husks)

With a corn husk (or if small, 2 slightly overlapped) take about ¼ cup of the dough, form into a potato-like shape, and place about 1″ from the bottom of the husk(s). Fold in the sides. Fold over the bottom, and fold over the tops. Continue with remaining tamalitos.

Place in a steamer and once the water is boiling, steam for 25 minutes. Check one of the tamalitos, if it is still soft when poked, steam for about 5 minutes more. The final consistency should be rather rubbery. Remove from heat and set aside. Can be steamed again, up to a day later, to warm.

Variations – add a small amount (¼ -½ cup) parboiled chopped vegetable and/or grated cheese

## Tamales with Filling and Sauce – Chuchitos

Chuchitos are essentially tamalitos, but enhanced with meat, sauce and vegetables. Lorocos are flower buds commonly used in southern Mexican and Central American cooking. Broccoli florets can be substituted.

Make about 2 lbs of masa by combining and mixing well with hands to make a rather stiff dough

> 4 cups masa harina (Maseca is a common brand available in the US)
>
> 2½ cups warm water

To the masa add, mix well and set aside

> ½ lb soft butter
>
> 2oz grated queso duro (romano cheese would be a good substitute)

Place in pot barely cover with water, bring to a boil, reduce heat and simmer until

> 2 lb chicken legs and thighs or 2 lb pork (Boston butt would be a good choice)
>
> 1 tsp salt

Allow to cool and cut into ½″ dice

Broil until skin somewhat blackened

> 1½ lb tomatoes
>
> 3 medium chiles pimientos

Roughly chop and sauté for a few minutes until somewhat thickened

> Roasted tomatoes and chiles
>
> 1 medium onion

As the sauce is thickening, add

> 4oz loroco or small pieces of broccoli florets

Soak in warm water

> Enough dried corn husks for the number of tamalitos you plan to make (1-2 each, depending on the size of the husks)

With a corn husk (or if small, 2 slightly overlapped) take about ¼ cup of the dough, place about 1″ from the bottom of the husk(s). Flatten out and place some meat and sauce on the dough. Form into a potato-like shape Fold in the sides. Fold over the bottom, and fold over the tops. Continue with remaining tamalitos.

Place in a steamer and once the water is boiling, steam for 25 minutes. Check one of the tamalitos, if it is still soft when poked, steam for about 5 minutes more. The final consistency should be rather rubbery. Remove from heat and set aside. Can be steamed again, up to a day later, to warm.

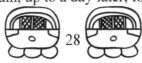

28

# Soups - Sopas

## Chicken Stew – Caldo de Pollo

Prepare some plain rice, using about 1½ cup dry or use one of our other more interesting rice recipes.

In a large pot, add, bring to a boil, reduce to a simmer and cook for 45 minutes or more until chicken is done

    3-4 lb chicken thighs and legs
    4 cloves peeled and smashed garlic cloves
    1 medium onion, halved
    4 whole peppercorns
    1 bay leaf
    Enough water to cover by about 2″

When the chicken is done, remove and set aside. Scoop out the other ingredients and discard. Add and simmer about 20 minutes

    1 medium sliced onion
    2 large peeled carrots, cut into, 1″-2″ slices
    2 large peeled potatoes quartered
    2 chayotes (güisquiles), peeled and cut into four large pieces
    3 coarsely chopped Roma tomatoes
    2-3 ears corn on the cob, cut into 2″-3″ inch thick pieces

While the vegetables are cooking, skin, debone and shred the chicken meat.

Add to the other vegetables and simmer 10 minutes more

    2 large zucchinis, cut into 2″-3″ inch thick pieces
    3 Tbsp chopped cilantro
    3 Tbsp chopped mint
    1-2 tsp salt, to taste

Add the shredded chicken meat and simmer a minute or so longer.

In this recipe, the vegetables and broth with meat are usually served separately. To serve, place 1-2 pieces of each vegetable on each plate along with some rice. Ladle the broth and meat into soup bowls. Have some lime wedges on hand – some like to add a little lime to their soup. Some hot tortillas on the side are always welcome.

## Hot Dog Soup – Sopa de Salchicha

Hot dogs are very popular in Guatemala. Slice into ¼″ rounds

    2 lb quality hot dogs

Thinly slice

    1 medium onion

Heat in a large saucepan
> 2 Tbsp butter

Sauté hot dogs and onion until lightly browned and add, bring to a boil, reduce to a simmer and cook about 10 minutes
> 6 cups water
> 1¼ cups rice
> 1 tsp pepper

Add, cover and cook for 10-20 minutes more until rice is done
> 4oz tomato paste

Add, mix well and bring up to heat
> 2 cups milk
> ½ cup crema

## Watercress Soup – Caldo de Berros

Coarsely chop
> 1 medium onion
> 1 carrot
> 1 medium zucchini
> 2 cloves garlic

Bring to a boil in a large saucepan
> 1½ qt chicken stock

Add chopped vegetables, cover and reduce to simmer for 10 minutes. Place in a blender, puree and return to the saucepan.

Before serving, coarsely chop
> 2 cups watercress

Bring the pureed stock and vegetables to a simmer. Add and cook covered for 3 minutes.
> Chopped watercress
> ¼ tsp nutmeg

Taste for salt and serve.

 32

# Seafood - Mariscos

## Carribean Style Shrimp – Camarones Caribe

Guatemala has a very small Caribbean coast but its influence is felt nationwide. Caribbean dishes tend to be rather spicy. Though we like really spicy food, this recipe has been toned down a bit – if you want the real experience, increase the quantity of pepper. Ingredient note – this recipe calls for tamarind purée – available in most Latin groceries or in Latin sections of supermarkets. If not available, half the amount of lime juice could be substituted.

Boil for about 10 minutes

    4 lb large shrimp

Optionally, peel the shrimp

Marinate for 2 hours

    Shrimp

    12oz pilsner style beer

    1½ tsp pepper

    1½ tsp cayenne

    2 tsp ground or finely chopped bay leaves

    2 tsp thyme

    2 tsp oregano

    ¼ tsp salt

In a small saucepan mix, bring to simmer and cook for 5 minutes, stirring occasionally

    ⅔ cup tamarind pure

    ¼ cup brown sugar

    2 Tbsp flour

    1 cup unsweetened coconut milk

In a large skillet with a lid, over low heat add

    ¼ cup olive oil

When the oil is reasonably hot add the shrimp and marinade, cover and cook for about 4 minutes. Flip over and cook about 4 minutes more. Be sure the shrimp is cooked through but not overcooked as the shrimp will become rubbery. Remove to a warm serving platter. Cover with the sauce and garnish with

    ¼ cup unsweetened grated coconut.

## Pasta and Shrimp with Pepián Sauce – Pasta al Pepián

Bring to a boil, reduce to a simmer and cook for 10 minutes

    1½ cups chicken stock

    1 clove smashed garlic

1 whole clove

In a hot, dry skillet toast, stirring frequently, until the sesame seeds have "popped" for a minute or so

    2oz sesame seeds

    2oz pumpkin seeds

Remove the seeds. In the same skillet, roast for about 5 minutes, tossing around frequently

    ½ lb ripe tomatoes

    2oz husked tomatillos (miltomates)

    1 chile ancho

    1 chile guajillo or cascabel

    1 corn tortilla, broken into pieces

Place the seeds in a blender and grind until powdery. Add the roasted tomatoes, etc. and the strained broth and blend until smooth.

Add to the skillet and over low heat cook for 2-3 minutes

    1 Tbsp olive oil

    1 Tbsp flour

Gradually whisk in the blended ingredients and simmer for 10 minutes. Off heat add

    1½ tsp basil

    1½ tsp ground or finely chopped rosemary

    1½ tsp oregano

    1½ tsp thyme

    ½ cup dry white wine

Sauté for 1-2 minutes until the shrimp is pink

    1 Tbsp olive oil

    ½ lb small to medium peeled shrimp

Peel and cut into ¼" dice. Boil until rather tender

    ¾ lb potatoes

Finely grate

    ¼ lb quality Parmesan

Coarsely grate

    ¼ lb mozzarella

Prepare al dente according to package instructions

    1 lb pasta of your choosing

While the pasta is cooking bring the sauce to a simmer, add and cook for 5 minutes

    Potatoes

    Shrimp

When al dente, drain the pasta and return to the pot with
> 1 Tbsp olive oil
> Grated Parmesan

Sauté for about a minute and add the sauce with other ingredients. When serving, sprinkle with grated mozzarella.

### Shrimp in Red Pepián Sauce – Pepián Rojo con Camarones

In a small saucepan warm
> 4 cups chicken stock

In a small dry skillet (preferably cast iron – other types may warp) toast for 2 minutes
> ½ cup sesame seeds

Remove seeds and heat, flipping around until softened
> 2-3 chilies anchos (pasas)

Remove chilies and lightly char
> 1 medium white onion, quartered

In a blender purée
> Seeds
> Chilies
> Onion
> 3 cloves garlic
> 4 tomatoes, quartered
> 5- 10 chiltepe peppers, or 1-2 seeded jalapeño peppers
> 5 sprigs cilantro
> ½ tsp salt
> ¼ cup of the chicken stock

In a large pot combine
> 2 julienned carrots
> 1 large zucchini, cut into ½″ dice
> 1 large chayote (qüisquil), seed removed and cut into ½″ dice
> Puréed ingredients
> Remaining chicken stock
> Enough water to cover

Bring to a boil, reduce to a simmer and cook uncovered for about 20 minutes until the vegetables are beginning to become tender. Add and simmer about 5 minutes more
> ¼ cup minced cilantro
> 1 lb medium shrimp, peeled and deveined

Taste and adjust for salt

Have lime wedges and more chopped cilantro on the side for additional flavor and rice and corn tortillas on the side for soaking up all the tasty broth.

## Spaghetti and Crab with Pepián Sauce – Espagueti y Cangrejo al Pepián

A dish particularly popular around the capital

Coarsely grate

        4oz mozzerella

Finely grate

        4oz parmesan

Bring to a boíl, reduce to a simmer and cook for 10 minutes

        1½ chicken stock

        1 clove garlic

        1 clove

Broil, turning as needed until somewhat blackened

        ½ lb ripe tomatoes

        2oz husked tomatillos (miltomates)

Toast in a skillet (preferably cast iron, to avoid warping or delamination of the pan)

        1 tortilla

Remove the tortilla and toast

        2oz sesame seeds

        2oz pumpkin seeds

Remove the seeds and toast until softened

        1 Chile Ancho (Pasa)

        1 Chile Guajillo (Guaque)

In a blender, pureé

        Chicken stock with garlic and clove discarded

        Tomatoes and tomatillos

        Toasted tortilla

        Toasted seeds

        Chiles with stems removed

Place in a small skillet and cook over low heat for 10 minutes. Add, stirring constantly and cook for 3 minutes more and set aside

        1 tsp flour

Cook until barely tender and drain

        ¾ lb potatoes, diced into ¼″ cubes

Sauté for 2 minutes
    1½ tsp olive oil
    ½ lb crabmeat
Add and sauté for about 5 minutes more
    Potatoes
    ½ cup dry white wine
    1½ tsp basil
    1½ tsp rosemary – finely chopped or ground
    1½ tsp oregano
    1½ tsp thyme
Cook according package directions and drain
    1 lb pasta
In a large skillet sauté
    1½ tsp olive oil
    Pasta
When hot add and stir well
    Sauce
    Crabmeat and potatoes
    Grated cheeses

## Tilapia with Chiltepe Sauce – Tilapia al Chiltepe

Chiltepe peppers are very common in Guatemala and most of Central America. They are small round or oval chilies about the size of small peas – they do pack a punch. If they are not available, jalapeños or serranos can be substituted.

Coarsely chop
    8oz husked tomatillos (miltomates)
    1 large clove garlic
    1 small onion
    20 chiltepes or 3 jalapeños or 4 serranos
Place in a saucepan bring to a boil, cover and simmer for 5 minutes
    Chopped vegetables
    ½ cup water
    ¼ tsp pepper
    ¼ tsp salt

Run the cooked ingredients through a blender for 1 minute and return to the saucepan. Add and simmer for 3 more minutes

    ½ tsp ground or finely chopped bay leaf

    ½ tsp thyme

    ¼ tsp pepper

    2 tsp vinegar

    1 Tbsp olive oil

Grate

    ¼-½ cup quality Parmesan

To a large skillet over medium heat, add

    2 Tbsp olive oil

When the oil is hot, sauté for about 2 minutes per side

    4 tilapia filets, 6oz-8oz each

Place on a warm serving platter, cover with sauce and grated Parmesan. Garnish with

    2-3 basil leaves per filet

40

# Poultry - Aves

## Chicken and Ribs Pepián – Pepián de Pollo y Costillas

Prepare some rice, using about 1½ cup dry.

Broil until slightly blackened on all sides

> 10 small or 5 large husked tomatillos (miltomates)
> 4 plum tomatoes
> 2 small peeled onions

Place in a blender

In a small dry skillet (preferably cast iron – other types may warp) toast 2-4 minutes until golden and popping.

> ¼ cup sesame seeds

Add to the blender

In the same skillet toast 7-8 minutes until golden and popping

> ¼ cup pumpkin seeds

Add to the blender

De-stem and in the same skillet toast 1-3 minutes until fragrant

> 1 chile ancho (pasa)
> 1 chile guajillo (guaque)

Remove seeds for a milder experience and add to the blender and blend until smooth, along with

> 4 cloves garlic
> 5 sprigs cilantro
> 1 tsp salt
> ¼ cup water (a little more may be needed)

In a large pot, bring to a boil, reduce to a simmer, cover and cook for 1 hour

> 1 lb pork short ribs, separated

Add and bring back to a boil, reduce to a simmer, cover again and simmer another 30 minutes

> 2-3 lb chicken legs and thighs
> 2 large carrots, peeled and cut into 4 pieces each
> 2 peeled, seed removed and quartered chayote (güísquil)

Add

> 2 medium potatoes, peeled and cut into 4 pieces each
> 2 large zucchini cut into thick slices

If needed, remove enough water so the ingredients in the pot are barely covered. Add the blended ingredients, return to a boil, reduce to a simmer and cook uncovered for 20 minutes or so, until the broth is thick.

To serve, place cooked rice in large bowls, about a ½ cup each. Ladle chicken and pork into bowls with plenty of vegetables and about ½-⅔ cup of broth. Sprinkle with cilantro and serve with warm corn tortillas.

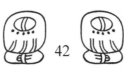

## Chicken in Beer Sauce – Pollo en Cerveza

Reduce to ½ cup
      1 cup chicken stock
Mix together
      2 Tbsp brown sugar
      1 Tbsp oregano
      2 tsp black pepper
      2 tsp onion salt
      1 finely chopped de-stemmed chile ancho (pasa)
Use the mixture to season
      8-10 small chicken thighs or equivalent
Add 2 Tbsp oil to a large skillet and brown in batches, adding more oil if needed
      Chicken thighs
When the last batch of thighs have been removed, add enough oil to skillet to make 2 Tbsp and sauté
      1 large thinly sliced onion
When the onion is beginning to brown, add and sauté
      1 large thinly sliced bell pepper
      2 thinly sliced carrots
      1 cup thinly sliced celery
After about 4 minutes more, add and cook 2-3 minutes more, stirring frequently
      1 Tbsp flour
Gradually add, stirring constantly to avoid lumps
      Reduced chicken broth
      12oz beer – dark is better
After the vegetables and sauce has come together, add
      Browned chicken
Cook for about 30 minutes until done.
Taste for salt and add if needed. Garnish with
      Chopped parsley

## Chicken Enchiladas Mexican Style – Enchiladas de Pollo Méxicanas

This recipe can also be made with beef or pork, just substitute for the chicken, though the poaching time will be longer
Coarsely grate
      ½ cup Oaxaca or mozzarella cheese

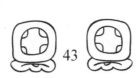

43

Using ½ lb tomatillo or tomato, prepare a batch of

> Green Tomatillo Sauce
>
> or
>
> Ranch Style Tomato Sauce

Poach until just done and shred

> ½ lb chicken breast

Preheat the oven to 350° F

Beat together

> ½ cup crema
>
> ½ cup milk

Film a skillet slightly larger than the tortillas with

> Oil

Fry until golden but still pliable, a few seconds per side, using more oil if needed. Transfer to paper towels to drain

> 1 lb corn tortillas

If doing this by yourself, fry about 5 tortillas at a time and proceed with the assembly. Repeat with remaining tortillas – you may have a few left over. With a helper, you can do this in an assembly line manner.

Place the tortillas on a work surface. Divide the shredded chicken evenly among the tortillas and roll up each like a cigar. Spread ⅓ cup of the sauce in a 13-by-9-by-2-inch glass baking dish. Arrange the enchiladas in 1 layer, seam-side down, snugly inside the dish. Pour the rest of the sauce over the enchiladas. Drizzle the cream mixture on top and sprinkle the cheese all over. Bake until the cheese is melted and starting to brown in spots, about 30 minutes. Serve immediately.

## Chicken in Chicha Sauce – Gallo en Chicha

Chicha is similar to beer though instead of malted barley, it's made with malted corn. The end result is a bit more crude than beer. A full flavored beer such a pale ale or some craft beers could be substituted.

The day before cut into pieces

> 1 small chicken

Season well with

> 1 Tbsp salt
>
> 1 tsp pepper

Cover and refrigérate

Make a batch of fresh pimento salad, with the addition or some sliced onion

The next day, bring to a boíl and reduce to a simmer

> 2½ cups chicken stock

Wipe the excess salt from the chicken

In a large skillet heat
    ¼ cup oil
Sauté the chicken in batches until browned on all sides and add to the simmering stock. Simmer for 35-45 minutes. Meanwhile in the skillet and oil used for the sautéed chicken cook until somewhat thickened
    ¼ cup chopped onion
    1 cup seeded and chopped tomatoes
    1 large clove chopped garlic
    ⅓ cup chopped raisins
    ¼ tsp cinnamon
    1 tsp coarsely ground pepper
When the chicken is done, add the sautéed ingredients and
    4 cloves
    1 cup chicha
Add salt if needed.
To serve, place in bowls and garnish with pimento salad with onions

## Chicken in Cream and Loroco Sauce – Pollo en Crema y Lorocos

Lorocos are flower buds commonly used in southern Mexican and Central American cooking. Broccoli florets can be substituted.
Finely chop
    1 medium onion
Coarsely chop
    2-3 Roma tomatoes
In a large saucepan brown
    1-2 Tbsp oil
    2 lb chicken pieces – legs and thighs are most typical
When the chicken is browned, add
    1 finely chopped clove garlic
Quickly add, so as not to burn the garlic
    ¾ cup chicken stock
Chopped onions and tomatoes
Reduce to a simmer, add and cover
    ½ cup loroco
When the chicken is done add and cook for a few minutes
    ¾ cup crema

## Chicken in Jocón Sauce I – Jocón de Pollo I

In a small saucepan simmer for about 10 minutes and drain
>8oz husked tomatillos (miltomates)

Enough water to cover

In a heavy pot or Dutch oven, sauté until browned on all sides and set aside
>¼ cup oil
>2 lb chicken legs and thighs

In the same pot and oil, toast for about 2 minutes
>1 medium chopped onion
>½ cup pumpkin seeds
>2 Tbsp sesame seeds

Remove onion and seeds and allow to cool somewhat. Add to a blender with
>2 cups chicken broth
>1 large sprigs cilantro
>1-2 cloves garlic
>1 tsp pepper

Purée until smooth and return to the pot along with the browned chicken pieces. Bring to a simmer and cook uncovered for 30 minutes. Taste for salt. Serve with rice and/or black beans (whole, refried or Frijolitos Fritos)

## Chicken in Jocón Sauce II-III – Jocón de Pollo II-III

See recipes for Beef and Pork I-II in Jocón Sauce in Meat, substituting chicken

## Chicken in Peanut Pepián – Pepián de Manía

This pepián features peanuts instead of seeds.

Cut into pieces, place in pot barely cover with water, bring to a boil, reduce heat and simmer until tender
>3 lb chicken legs and thighs
>1 tsp salt

Toast in a skillet (preferably cast iron, to avoid warping or delamination of the pan)
>2oz pumpkin seed
>2oz sesame seed

In the same pan lightly roast, remove and add to seeds
>1 chile ancho (pasa)
>1 chile guajillo (guaque)

Broil until somewhat blackened
>½ lb tomatoes

46

½ lb husked tomatillos (miltomates)

Place the seeds, chilies, tomatoes and tomatillos in a blender along with

 ½ tsp cinnamon

 1 clove

 2 allspice berries

 ½ tsp black pepper

 1 lb roasted peanuts

Blend until smooth, place in a bowl and gradually add the broth from the chicken. Add the thickened broth back to the chicken.

Before serving, reheat if needed and add

 1 cup chopped cilantro

 Salt to taste

## Chicken in Red Pepián Sauce – Pepián Colorado de Pollo

There a many variations of Mayan pepián sauces. The one thing they all have in common are ground toasted seeds.

Cut into pieces, place in pot barely cover with water, bring to a boil, reduce heat and simmer until tender

 3 lb chicken legs and thighs

 1 tsp salt

Turn off heat, remove chicken and set aside.  Reduce the cooking broth to 1½ cups

Place in a pot, cover with water. Bring to boil and cook until vegetables are tender.

 1 chayote, mirliton (güisquil), seed removed and cut into ½″ dice

 2 large carrots, peeled and cut into ½″ dice

 1 lb small boiling potatoes, peeled

 ½ lb green beans, halved

As the vegetables become tender, remove with slotted spoon and set aside.

Broil, turning occasionally until skin blistered and somewhat blackened

 1 lb ripe tomatoes

 1 red bell pepper

Bring some water to a boil in a small saucepan, turn off heat, add and allow to cook for about 10 minutes

 ½ lb husked tomatillos (miltomates)

Toast in a skillet (preferably cast iron, to avoid warping or delamination of the pan)

 4 ounces sesame seeds

 4 ounces pumpkin seeds

 2 slices white bread, cubed

Place in a blender and blend until pasty
> The seeds and bread
> ½ cup of the reserved chicken cooking broth

Add the tomatoes (stem core removed), bell pepper (seeded and deveined), tomatillos and remaining chicken broth to the blender and puree.

Before serving, place the pureed mixture, vegetables and chicken in pot, bring to a boil, reduce to a simmer, and cook until hot. Add salt if needed. Typically served with rice.

## Chicken Kaq'ik Style I – Kaq'ik de Pollo I

There are many Mayan dishes characterized by a sauce called kaq'ik. Though similar, they vary. Pork and less commonly beef, can be substituted for the chicken.

In a large saucepan, bring to boil, reduce to a simmer and cook until chicken is done
> 5 lb chicken legs and thighs
> One large bulb garlic – no need to peel or chop
> ½ tsp cinnamon
> Enough water to cover

Remove the chicken and set aside. Discard the garlic and water.

In a large skillet cook until softened
> 1 lb husked tomatillos (miltomates)
> 10-15 Roma tomatoes
> 4 chiles guajillos (guaques)
> 10 cloves
> 5-10 sprigs cilantro – depending on size

When softened, purée the vegetables and spices in a blender. Place the puréed ingredients in the saucepan used to cook the chicken, add back the chicken and add
> 5-10 sprigs chopped mint – depending on size
> 5-10 sliced green onions – depending on size
> 1 tsp ground annatto (achiote)
> Salt to taste

## Chicken Kaq'ik Style II – Kaq'ik de Pollo II

There are many Mayan dishes characterized by a sauce called kaq'ik. Though similar, they vary. Pork and less commonly beef, can be substituted for the chicken.

In a large saucepot cook with enough water to cover, for 20 minutes, until almost done

    4-5 lbs chicken thighs and legs, separated

    8 large cloves garlic, slightly smashed

    1-2 cinnamon sticks or ½ tsp ground cinnamon

    10 cloves

When done remove the chicken and discard the water and other ingredients. Return the chicken to the saucepot.

In a large skillet, cook until tender

    10 Roma tomatoes, cut in half

    1 lb husked tomatillos (miltomates), cut in half

    5-7 scallions, coarsely chopped

    5 large sprigs cilantro, coarsely chopped

    4 chiles guajillos (guaques)

Purée

    Tender vegetables

    2 tsp ground annatto (achiote) – paprika may be substituted

    1 tsp salt

Pass though a coarse strainer into the saucepot with chicken. Simmer 5-15 minutes until chicken is done.

Optionally garnish with

    ¼ cup chopped mint

## Chicken Kaq'ik Style III – Kaq'ik de Pollo III

There is an assortment of Mayan dishes characterized by a sauce called kaq'ik. Though similar, kaq'ik sauces vary. Pork and less commonly beef, can be substituted for the chicken.

Cut into pieces, place in pot barely cover with water, bring to a boil, reduce heat and simmer until tender

    3 lb chicken legs and thighs

    1 tsp salt

Turn off heat, remove chicken and set aside.  Reserve the cooking broth.

In a skillet combine and gently cook until onions are tender

    2 lbs coarsely chopped ripe tomatoes

    ¼ lb husked tomatillos (miltomates)

    2  chiles guajillas (guaques)

    2 chiles serranos or 1 chile jalapeño (remove seeds and veins for less heat)

    3 medium onions cut into eighths

    2 medium cloves garlic

Puree in a blender

     The cooked vegetables

     2 slices white bread, broken into pieces

     1 tsp black pepper

     Some of the broth from cooking the chicken – enough to blend

Add the remaining stock and blend a bit more. Return the blended mixture to the pot and add

     3 sprigs mint

     3 sprigs cilantro

     1 Tbsp ground annatto (achiote)

     Salt to taste

     The cooked chicken pieces

Before serving, bring to a boil, reduce heat and simmer for 10 minutes. Serve with tamalitos and/or rice.

## Chicken Stew with Peas and Mint – Caldo de Pollo con Arvejas y Menta

In a large pot sauté until onions are beginning to brown

     2 Tbsp olive oil

     1 large chopped onion

Add and bring to a boil, reduce heat to simmer and cook for about 20 minutes until chicken breasts are nearly done

     3 cloves minced garlic

     2 chicken breast halves, preferably bone in

     2 qt chicken stock

     1 cup coarsely diced carrots

Remove the chicken and set aside. Add and simmer 30 minutes

     1 15oz can rinsed and drained beans, preferably white beans

     ½ cup rice

     ½ small head chopped cabbage

     1 cup fresh or frozen peas

     1 tsp pepper

     ½ tsp salt

In the meantime shred the chicken into bite size pieces.

Add to the soup and simmer about 5 minutes more

     Shredded chicken

     ¼ cup mint leaves, rinsed and chopped

Taste for salt. Serve along with crusty bread or hot tortillas.

## Chicken with Onion – Pollo Encebollado

Place in a large pot, brown
>   ¼ cup oil
>   ¼ cup olive oil
>   3-4 chicken thighs and legs
>   1 tsp salt
>   1 tsp pepper

Add, bring to a boil, reduce to a simmer for 45 minutes or more until chicken is done.
>   ½ cup dry white wine
>   ½ cup vinegar
>   1 cup coarsely chopped tomato
>   1½ cups thinly sliced onion
>   4 bay leaves
>   4 coarsely chopped tomatoes
>   Some water, if needed during the cooking process

As the chicken is nearing completion, taste for salt.

## Hen Stew – Caldo de Gallina

A gallina is a hen, larger and tougher than a chicken. So if you opt for a regular chicken, cooking times probably could be reduced significantly.

Slice the stem ends off, and quarter
>   3 large roma tomatoes

Cut widthwise the white part into 3 pieces
>   1 large leek

Place in the cavity of the hen
>   2 scallions
>   1 of the tomatoes
>   1 piece of leek

In a pot with a lid, large enough for the bird, add and bring to a boil
>   Hen
>   Remaining tomatoes and leek pieces
>   4 scallions
>   Enough water to cover by about 4″
>   2 tsp salt

51

Reduce to a simmer, cover and cook 2-3 hours for a hen – 45 minutes-1 hour for a chicken. Test for doneness by stabbing a thick part with a sharp knife. A hen should be rather tender. For a chicken, the juices should run clear. Remove the hen and discard the vegetables in the broth.

Add to the broth and cook uncovered about 30 minutes more, until tender

> 2 carrots, peeled and cut into chunks
>
> 3 medium potatoes, peeled and cut into large cubes
>
> 1 chayote, with seed removed, cut in chunks (optional)

While the carrots, etc. are cooking, cut the hen into serving pieces, discarding the vegetables in the cavity. Broil both sides of the chicken pieces until browned.

Remove the vegetables from the broth and set aside. Add to the broth and simmer about 5 minutes

> 1 large sprig chopped mint

Serve the chicken with the vegetables on the side, and the broth in soup bowls.

## Stewed Chicken – Pollo Guisado

Separate thighs from legs

> 3 lb chicken leg quarters

Slice

> 1 large onion

Coarsely chop

> 8 Roma tomatoes
>
> 3 large cloves garlic

Dice to ¾"

> 4 medium peeled potatoes
>
> 4 medium peeled carrots

In a large pot brown, turning the chicken occasionally to brown on all sides

> 2 Tbsp oil
>
> Chicken pieces

Add, cover pot and cook for 5 minutes more over low heat

> ½ tsp cinnamon
>
> 6 bay leaves
>
> 1 tsp thyme

Add and cook uncovered over low heat for 15-25 minutes until the chicken is done

> 1½ cups chicken stock
>
> 1½ Tbsp sugar
>
> ½ tsp salt
>
> Sliced, chopped and diced vegetables

Add and cook 5-10 minutes more
        ¼ cup vinegar
Taste and add salt if needed.
Serve with hot tortillas and sliced avocados sprinkled with lime juice.

 54

# Meat - Carnes

## Beef or Pork in Jocón Sauce I – Jocón de Res o Cerdo I

There is an assortment of Mayan dishes characterized by a sauce called Jocón. Though similar, Jocón sauces vary. Chicken may be substituted.

In a medium saucepan, barely cover with water and simmer until the meat is done to your liking

> 1 lb sirloin tip or other medium tender beef or pork such as Boston butt
> 1 onion, coarsely chopped
> 1 tomato, coarsely chopped
> 1 clove garlic, smashed
> 1 tsp salt

Remove and thinly slice the beef or cut into ¾″ cubes. Reserve the cooking liquid.

Purée

> 4 scallions
> ¼ lb husked tomatillos (miltomates)
> 4 large sprigs cilantro
> 2-4 jalapeños, depending on your taste
> 1-2 cloves garlic
> 2 cups strained broth from meat

Melt

> 2 Tbsp butter

Add cooking slowly for about 2 minutes

> 2 Tbsp breadcrumbs

Gradually add, stirring well

> Puréed ingredients

When somewhat thickened add the cooked meat and cook until all is hot.

Serve with rice

## Beef or Porkin Jocón Sauce II – Jocón de Res o Cerdo

There is an assortment of Mayan dishes characterized by a sauce called Jocón. Though similar, Jocón sauces vary. Chicken may be substituted.

Combine

> 1 lb sirloin tip or other medium tender beef or pork such as Boston butt
> 1 quartered onion
> 1 roughly chopped tomato
> 1 large clove smashed garlic
> 1 tsp salt

Enough water to cover

56

Bring to a boil, reduce to a simmer and cook until tender 40 minutes – 1½ hours. Drain and cut into serving size pieces. Reserve the broth – you will need some for the sauce.

Purée in a blender or food processor

2 large clove garlic

¼ lb husked tomatillos (miltomates)

2 large sprigs cilantro

2 peppers – anywhere from bell peppers to Hungarian peppers, depending on your taste for heat

2-4 scallions – depending on size

2 cups of the cooking broth

Heat until bubbling

2 Tbsp butter

Add the puréed ingredients, add and cook until thickened

2 Tbsp fine breadcrumbs

½ tsp salt

1 tsp pepper

Add the meat and cook until heated

## Beef or Pork Kaq'ik Style

See recipes I-III for Chicken Kaq'ik in Poultry substituting meat

## Beef or Pork Enchiladas Mexican Style – Enchiladas de Res o Cerdo Méxicanas

See recipe for Chicken Enchiladas in Poultry substituting meat

## Beef Stew I – Caldo de Res

Prepare a recipe of Pico de Gallo (Chirmól)

Cut into ¾″ cubes

2 lbs beef chuck

Coarsely dice

1 tomato

1 medium onion

3 celery stalks

1 bell pepper

1 lb potato

1 small cabbage

1 peeled carrot

2 large cloves garlic

3 chayotes (güisqiles)

1 peeled cassava (yucca) root (optional)

Scrape kernels from

3 ears of corn – or substitute 2-3 cups frozen corn

Heat in a large soup pot until almost smoking

2 Tbsp olive oil

Brown the beef well on all sides, in batches if necessary to avoid crowding. If done in batches add back the first batch(es) of beef and the vegetables. Add enough water to almost cover vegetables. On high heat, bring to boil. Reduce heat to simmer and add

½ tsp ground coriander

½ tsp ground cumin

½ tsp ground annatto (achiote) – paprika may be substituted

1 tsp salt

Simmer until beef is tender. Add salt to taste.

Serve Pico de Gallo on the side to spice it up according to the diners' taste.

## Beef Stew II – Caldo de Res

Brown well

Enough oil to cover bottom of stockpot

1 lb stewing beef, cut into ¾″ cubes

2 lbs meaty soup bones

½ tsp salt

When brown, pour off oil and add

1 qt beef broth

Enough water to cover by 1″

½ lb cassava (yucca) root, peeled and diced

Bring to a boil, reduce to a simmer and cook until meat is somewhat tender. In the meantime prepare the vegetables

2 large carrots, peeled and cut into ¾″ pieces

1 lb pumpkin or other firm squash seeded and cut into ¾″ cubes

2 cobs of corn, quartered

1 chayote (güisquil), seed removed and cut into ¾″ cubes

1 lb boiling potatoes, peeled and cut into ¾″ cubes

1 medium turnip, peeled and cut into ¾″ cubes

Add the vegetables to the simmering beef – add water if needed to cover. Bring to a boil, reduce to a simmer, and cook until vegetables are tender.

Before serving, remove bones, return the meat from the bones to the soup and reheat if needed. Then add

    1 cup chopped cilantro

    Salt to taste

## Coastal Style Pork Stew – Carne Guisada de Marrano Estilo CostaSur

Cut into 16 or so pieces

    3 lb Boston butt or other somewhat fatty pork

Finely chop

    2-3 medium ripe tomatoes

    ½ cup husked tomatillos (miltomates)

    1 small onion

    1 chile ancho (pasa)

Thinly slice

    1 chile jalapeño

In a large pot, cover and cook slowly for 15-20 minutes to release fat in meat

    1 Tbsp oil

    Pork pieces

Remove cover, increase heat and brown the meat on all sides. When meat is browned, reduce heat and add

    Chopped and sliced vegetables

    2 tsp thyme

    2 large bay leaves

    1 tsp salt

    ½ tsp pepper

    ½ cup water

Mix well, cover and cook over low heat for about 30 minutes, until the pork is tender

## Guatemalan Fajitas – Fajitas Chapines

Prepare a marinade by combining

    1½ cups beer

    ½ cup olive oil

    4 finely chopped garlic cloves

    Juice of 2 large limes

    2 tsp pepper

    1 Tbsp chopped cilantro

    ½ tsp cayenne pepper

Cut into ¼ "-⅓" strips

1½-2 lbs skirt steak or flank steak
Add to the marinade and allow to marinate for 1-2 hours
Broil or roast until mostly blackened on all sides
     4 chiles poblanos (chiles pimientos)
Place in a plastic bag for about 10 minutes, rinse off most of the black and slice into ⅛″ strips
Thinly slice in rings
     4 large onions
     2 chiles poblanos in addition to the roasted ones (chiles pimientos)
Drain the marinated meat
In a large skillet, heat
¼ cup olive oil
Sauté over high heat, stirring often, until lightly browned and place in a large bowl
     ½ of the sliced onions and chiles
Repeat with the other half of the onions and chiles
If needed, add to the skillet
     1-2 Tbsp olive oil
Sauté to your preference of doneness
     ½ of the drained meat
Add to the sautéed vegetable. Repeat with the other half. Add the roasted chile strips and mix well.
Serve with corn and/or flour tortillas.

## Guatemalan Skirt Steak – Hilachas

Place in pot, barely cover with water, bring to a boil, reduce heat and simmer covered for ½ hour.
     1 lb boneless skirt or beef flank
     ½ tsp salt
     1 large clove garlic
Remove. When cooled tear into shreds and set aside.
In pot of boiling water, cook until rather tender
     1 lb boiling potatoes, peeled and sliced into ¼″ rounds
Refresh with cold water, drain and set aside
In the potato cooking pot, combine and cook over medium heat until the onion is tender
     1 lb ripe tomatoes, chopped
     ¼ lb husked tomatillos (miltomates)
     2 small or 1 large red bell peppers, seeded, deveined and coarsely chopped
     1 medium onion, coarsely chopped
     1 large clove garlic

½ tsp ground black pepper
½ tsp sugar
½ tsp salt
Have ready
      1 cup rich beef stock
Combine in a blender and puree
      Cooked tomatoes, onions, etc.
      Beef broth
Before serving, combine in a pot, bring to a boil, reduce to a simmer and cook for 15 minutes
      Blended sauce
      Shredded beef
      Boiled potatoes
      1 onion, finely chopped
Add salt if needed. Serve with rice and/or tamalitos.

## Pork Chops – Chuletas

Prepare a sauce as follows
Thinly slice
      1½ lb onions
Melt and cook covered very slowly, until the onions are soft, but not browned
      3 Tbsp butter
      Onions
Uncover, add and cook slowly for several minutes, stirring frequently
      2 Tbsp flour
Gradually whisk in and simmer for a few minutes until thickened
      2 cups hot chicken stock
Taste and add salt, if needed
Preheat oven to 300°F
Brown in a large skillet in batches so as not to crowd
      2 Tbsp butter
      1 Tbsp oil
      10 thin (¼″) pork chops
Place the browned pork chops in a large baking dish, cover with sauce. Cover the dish with foil and bake in preheated oven for 45 minutes.

## Ribs Steamed in Plantain Peels – Costillas Tapadas

This recipe calls for pork ribs. A pound of meaty ribs, about 3-5 ribs depending on size, are cut widthwise into 1½"-2" sections – have your butcher do this with a saw or whack them into pieces with an axe, as the ladies in the market do here. Baby back ribs or short ribs could be substituted.

Slice

> 8 medium Roma tomatoes
> 2 medium onions (preferably white)

Rinse well

> 4 ripe plantains (skin should me mostly black)

Carefully peel the plantains, reserving the peels – you may not need all of the peels. Slice each plantain lengthwise and widthwise into 3 sections yielding 6 pieces each.

Cut into 1-2 rib sections

> 1 lb pork ribs as described above

In a heavy pot, cover the bottom with plantain peels, outer side down. Drizzle with

> ¼ cup oil

Place a meager layer of ribs, followed by plantain pieces, onion and tomato. Sprinkle lightly with salt and pepper. Repeat until the ingredients are exhausted. Cover with plantain peels, outer side up. Add

> 2 cups water

Bring to a boil, reduce to a simmer and cook slowly until the ribs are tender.


## Steak with Tomato and Onion – Bistec con Tomate y Cebolla

Other than in some upscale steakhouses, steaks in Guatemala (and México for that matter) tend to be rather thin.

Reduce to ¼ cup

> 1 cup chicken stock

Slice the stem end off of

> 3 large, ripe Roma tomatoes

Place in a saucepan and cook for 5 minutes

> Tomatoes
> ½ cup water

Allow to cool and coarsely chop.

> Slice ¼"-⅜" thick
> 1 lb reasonably tender beef

Lightly season beef with salt and pepper. In a large skillet over medium heat add

> 2 Tbsp oil

Sauté the beef until browned on both sides, in batches if needed. Then add and brown
  1 medium thinly sliced onion
Add and cook about 3 minutes more
  1 clove finely minced garlic
  Chopped tomatoes
  Reduced chicken stock
Taste for salt.

### Stewed Beef – Carne Guisada

In a large saucepan, combine, bring to a boil, reduce to a simmer and cook about 30 minutes or more until the meat is tender.
  1 lb semi-tender beef, cut into ¾″ cubes
  1 large sliced carrot
  2 medium potatoes, cut to a ½″ dice
  8oz tomato paste
  1½ cups beef broth
  1 tsp cumin
  ½ tsp dry mustard
  1 tsp salt
  1 tsp pepper
Before serving add more salt and/or pepper to taste if needed

### Stuffed Pork Loin – Lomo de Cerdo Relleno

Cut ½″ deep lengthwise and carefully continue to cut lengthwise to create a ½″ thick slab
  2 lb lean pork loin
Rub the pork with a mixture of
  1 tsp pepper
  1 tsp salt
Combine and mix well
  2 lb lean ground beef
  ¼ cup flour
  1 Tbsp dry wine
  3 chopped tomatoes
  3 finely chopped onions
  2 cloves minced garlic
  ½ cup diced carrot

½ cup diced potato
½ cup thinly sliced green beans
½ cup peas
1 tsp finely chopped or ground bay leaves
1 tsp pepper
½ tsp ground nutmeg
¼ tsp ground anise
½ tsp thyme
¼ tsp cumin
1 tsp salt

In a large skillet sauté until the beef is done
6 Tbsp butter
Ground beef mixture

Spread the sautéed mixture over the pork slab and roll up like a jelly roll. Tie with cotton twine in 4-5 places to hold together.

Preheat oven to 350°F

In a Dutch oven heat until almost smoking
4 Tbsp lard or oil

Fry the filled pork on all sides until brown. Place in preheated oven and roast until internal temperature reaches 170°F

## Tex-Mex Style Fajitas – Fajitas Tex-Mex

Much easier than the traditional Guatemalan style, though you will need to prepare and have on hand several sauces and toppings.

Over high heat in a pan large enough not to crowd, brown
3 Tbsp olive oil
1½ lbs skirt steak or other thinly sliced steak

Add and cook partially covered for at least 20-30 minutes (until the liquid has evaporated)
7 large cloves minced garlic
7 minced green onions
1 tsp oregano
12oz beer

More beer can be added periodically to extend the cooking time and tenderness. Serve with corn and/or flour tortillas, rajas de chili poblano, guacamole, crumbled queso fresco, and several different salsas.

# Vegetables - Vegetales

65

## Fried Plantains – Plátanos Fritos

Peel and quarter, lengthwise and in half
>   4 ripe plantains – a ripe plantain is black or nearly black

In a large skillet over medium low heat
>   2 Tbsp oil

Fry the plantain quarters until lightly browned on each side.

## Fried Plantains with Bean Filling – Frituras de Plátano y Frijól

Mildly sweet and savory. A vegetable, protein and starch – all in one.
In a large pot, bring to a boil, reduce to a simmer and cook 20-25 minutes until fork tender
>   2½ lb ripe plantains, ends removed and cut into 3 pieces
>   Enough water to cover

Allow to cool and peel
With a potato masher or fork mash, leaving some texture
>   1 16oz can rinsed and drained black beans

In a medium skillet sauté for about a minute
>   2 Tbsp oil
>   ⅓ cup finely chopped onion
>   1 clove minced garlic

Add the mashed beans and cook until thickened – 3-5 minutes
In a large bowl beat until somewhat fluffy – an electric mixer may be helpful
>   Peeled plantains

Stir in
>   ⅓ cup flour
>   ¼ tsp salt

With damp hands (to prevent sticking) form quarter cups of the plantain mixture into 3″ patties. Slightly indent a patty and place about 2 Tbsp of the beans in the indentation. Cover with another patty and lightly mash together the edges. Repeat with the remaining patties and beans.
Preheat oven to 200°F
In a large deep saucepan or fryer (we use a wok) heat to 350°F
>   2½ cups oil

Place several of the patties in the hot oil for 1-2 minutes per side, until golden. Drain on paper towels and place in warm oven. Repeat with remaining patties, allowing the oil to return to 350°F between batches. Serve hot.

## Refried Beans – Frijoles Revueltos

There's nothing wrong with refried beans out of the can – just heat and serve. For a tastier experience, try this recipe.

In a medium skillet sauté slowly

> 3 Tbsp oil
> 1 medium sliced onion

Grate

> ½ cup Parmesan (per can of beans) – crumbled queso fresco works well too

Remove and discard the onions used to season the oil. Add

> 1-2 16oz cans refried beans

Heat, scraping frequently, until they start to come together. Remove from heat and beat in

> Cheese

## Stuffed Chilies in Tomato Sauce – Chiles Rellenos en Salsa de Tomate

In Guatemala, chiles pimientos are very common – they are usually red, but are sometimes green. A close substitute would be a Mexican chile poblano, almost always green.

Prepare by cutting off the stem end and removing most of the seeds

> 12 medium (about 5"-6" long) chiles pimientos

Combine and mix well

> 1½ lb lean ground beef
> 1 egg
> ⅔ cup breadcrumbs
> 3 coarsely diced Roma tomatoes
> ½ finely chopped onion
> 1 tsp salt
> ½ tsp pepper

Stuff the chiles with the mixture.

Place in a saucepan with enough water to barely cover and cook until tender

> 7 Roma tomatoes cut in half
> 1 tsp salt

Purée tomatoes and the water in a blender or food processor

In a large skillet with cover or Dutch oven sauté until tender

> 1 Tbsp oil
> ½ finely chopped onion
> 2 cloves finely chopped garlic

Add the tomato purée and cook. Add the stuffed peppers, cover and cook slowly for 20-30 minutes. Serve with steamed rice or mashed potatoes.

## Stuffed Zucchini – Zuchinis Rellenos

Rinse well
>3 medium zucchinis

Bring to a boil in a saucepan large enough to accommodate the zucchinis
>Water
>1 Tbsp salt

Add the zucchinis and cook until slightly fork tender. Drain in a colander and allow to cool a bit.
Chop
>1 medium onion

Coarsely grate and add to the onion
>1 medium carrot

Coarsely grate into a separate bowl
>¼ lb cheddar

Preheat oven to 350°
In a skillet large enough to accommodate the vegetable, sauté until the onion is slightly browned
>2 Tbsp butter
>1 Tbsp oil
>Onions and carrots

Add most of the grated cheese and stir well
Cut the zucchinis in half, scrape out the seeds and fill with the sautéed mixture. Place on a baking sheet, sprinkle with remaining cheese. Bake in preheated oven about 15 minutes until slightly browned.

## Tomatoes Stuffed with Cheese – Tomates Manzanos con Queso

In Guatemala, Roma tomatoes are much more common than the round variety. They call the round variety Tomates Manzanos (Apple Tomatoes).
Mix together
>1½ tsp basil
>1½ tsp oregano
>1½ tsp finely chopped bay leaf
>½ tsp pepper

Coarsely grate
>½ cup flavorful mozzarella or asiago

Sauté for about 30 seconds
      1 Tbsp olive oil
      1 large clove finely minced garlic
Add and sauté 3 minutes more
      ½ lb finely (¼″) diced zucchini
      ¼ tsp salt
Add and sauté 3 minutes more
      ⅔ cup corn kernels
Preheat oven to 350°F
Cut about ⅜″ off the top of (reserve the tops)
      6 medium to large ripe tomatoes
With a small spoon, scrape out the seeds and membranes and discard. Place tomatoes in a baking dish. To each tomato, add
      ¼ tsp olive oil
      ½ tsp spice mixture
      2 tsp vegetable mixture
      2 tsp cheese
Continue adding the vegetables and cheese until exhausted. Sprinkle each tomato with
      Pinch of thyme
Place the reserved tops on the tomatoes and place in the preheated oven for 15 minutes. Remove the tops and bake for 2 more minutes.

70

# Beverages - Bebidas

## Bloody Mary – Bloody Mary

Although the name of this cocktail easily translates to "María Sangrosa" – it is never called that – just say Bloody Mary with a bit of a Spanish accent.

In a pitcher combine
- 1 cup vodka
- 2 cups tomato juice
- Juice of 1 lemon and 1 lime – yielding ⅓ to ½ cup
- ½-1 tsp Tabasco
- ¾ tsp Worcestershire
- ¼ tsp celery salt
- ¼ tsp pepper

## Hangover Cure Consommé – Consomé Quita Goma

Created by students at Universidad de San Carlos de Guatemala (USAC) – the fourth oldest university in the Americas

Coarsely chop
- 1 medium onion
- 2 Roma tomatoes

Finely chop
- 1 chile Serrano or 1 small jalapeño or 4 chiltepes

Bring to a boil
- 2 qt chicken stock

Add the chopped vegetables and
- Juice of 1 lime
- 1-2 Tbsp Worcestershire sauce, or to taste

## Margaritas - Margaritas

A lot of the bad reputation tequila has is because many contain cheap alcohol instead of pure tequila. One of the most popular brands in the US is one of the guilty parties. Always look for the designation 100% Agave – it's not necessarily more expensive.

Combine
- 1 part Tequila
- 1 part freshly squeezed lime juice
- ½ part Triple Sec

You can make these frozen in a blender, but we find they are best are served straight up. Use a cocktail shaker. Fill with ice and mixture, shake and pour into cocktail glass. You can rim the glass with salt if you like.

## Rum and Pepsi – Ron y Pepsi

Rum is the national drink of Guatemala. Pepsi is more popular than CocaCola here. If you bring some rum (.75 L or 1.75L) and some Pepsi to a party, the party will not disband until all the rum is gone.

A note to visitors – Pepsi, 7Up and other carbonated beverages are generically called Aguas (Waters). If you really want some water, you need to ask for Agua Pura (Pure Water).

To serve

> A bottle of rum
> Some Pepsi and/or 7Up
> Ice is optional, Guatemalans don't seem to care if it's cold or not

Pass the bottles around and allow the guests to make them as strong or weak as they like. As the evening progresses, less "Agua" and more rum will be the norm.

## Sweetened Rice with Milk – Arroz con Leche

Here, most of the tiendas sell arroz quebrada – "broken rice". To make your own, take regular long grain rice and pulse a few times in a food processor – just to break, not create a rice flour.

In a large saucepan, bring to a boil and reduce to low

> 2 cups water
> ½ lb arroz quebrada
> ½ tsp cinnamon

When the rice becomes somewhat mushy, add

> ½ cup sugar
> ½ cup raisins
> ½ tsp salt

Cook slowly until thickened.

73

## Thick Hot Corn Beverage – Atol de Elote

There are countless varieties of atol in Guatemala. Rarely made at home – most frequently delivered by ladies wearing traditional Mayan clothing who go door-to-door. On the opposite side of the spectrum is the dried powder product, the most popular brand being Incaparina, sold in supermarkets that is added to boiling water. Here is a typical homemade version – yields about 6 cups.

In a blender or food processor, pulse until mostly liquefied, but still having texture.

> 2 cups yellow corn kernels – fresh or frozen
> ½ cup water

In a saucepan bring to a boil and reduce to a simmer

> Corn
> 2½ cups water
> 1 cup milk
> 1 cup sugar
> 1 tsp cinnamon
> ½ tsp salt

Cook for about 10 minutes and serve with a bit of cinnamon sprinkled on top.

# Desserts - Postres

## Banana Bread – Pastel de Banano

Banana bread is very common here, especially on the shores of Lake Atitlán. We make this when we find overripe, almost rotten bananas on clearance.

Beat until smooth and set aside

> 4 cups very ripe (almost rotten) bananas

Cream

> 1 stick butter
>
> 1 cup sugar

Add, beating well

> 2 eggs

Stir in

> ½ tsp salt
>
> 1 tsp baking soda
>
> 2 cups flour
>
> 1 cup chopped pecans

Add

> The beaten bananas

Bake in loaf pan at 350° for one hour and 15 minutes to an hour and a half, use toothpick to test for doneness.

## Buñuelos

A doughnut-like confection

Prepare a syrup by combining in a small saucepan, bringing to a boil and cooking for 5 minutes

> 1 cup water
>
> ½ cup sugar
>
> ½ tsp cinnamon
>
> 1 tsp vanilla

Combine

> 2 cups flour
>
> 2 tsp baking powder

In a larger saucepan, scald

> 1 cup milk
>
> ¼ tsp salt
>
> 1 tsp vanilla

 76

After 1 minute remove from heat and add, beating vigorously
>Flour mixture

Add one at a time, beating well
>2 eggs

Cover and allow to rest for at least 1 hour.

When ready to serve, heat to 350° in deep fryer – we use a wok
>Enough oil for deep frying

When oil is hot, place heaping tablespoons of dough in the hot oil – this may need to be done in batches so as not to crowd – be sure to allow the oil to return temperature before frying subsequent batches. When golden brown, remove to paper towels to drain. Serve with syrup prepared previously.

## Carrot Cake – Pastel de Zanahoria

Carrot cake is just as popular in Guatemala as elsewhere.

Combine and mix well
>2 cups flour
>2 tsp baking soda
>1 tsp salt
>1 tsp cinnamon
>Add and mix well
>3 cups grated carrot
>1½ cups chopped nuts

Preheat oven to 350°

In a separate bowl, combine
>2 cups sugar
>1½ cups oil

Beat in one by one
>4 eggs

Stir into the dry ingredients. Place in an appropriate sized baking dish and bake in the preheated oven for 45 minutes to 1 hour until a sharp knife inserted comes out clean.

As in other carrot cake recipes, this is typically frosted, though we prefer it as it is. To make frosting, beat until fluffy
>6 Tbsp butter
>4oz cream cheese
>2 tsp vanilla

Stir in
>2 cups powdered sugar

## Custard Filled Éclairs – Repollitos con Dulce de Leche

Bring to a boil

>1 cup water
>
>1 stick (4oz) butter

Reduce heat to low and gradually whisk in

>1 cup flour

Cook for a few minutes, whisking frequently. Remove from heat and allow to cool for about 10 minutes. Preheat oven to 300°.

Whisk in one by one

>4 eggs

Place tablespoons of batter/dough on cookie sheets (preferably non-stick), leaving plenty of space between them. Place in preheated oven for 15-20 until golden brown. Remove to cooling racks.

Combine and stir well

>4 tsp cornstarch
>
>½ cup water

In a heavy saucepan, heat until nearly boiling

>2 cups milk
>
>½ tsp cinnamon

Reduce heat and whisk in

>Dissolved cornstarch
>
>2 egg yolks
>
>½ cup sugar
>
>1 tsp butter

Continue cooking until thickened, allow to cool somewhat.

Cut ¼″-½″ from the tops of the pastries. If doughy, scoop out most of the dough from the lower part and fill with the cream sauce made earlier.

Top with either

>Powdered sugar or melted semi-sweet chocolate

## Custard Filled Fried Pies – Empanadas de Leche

Combine

>3 Tbsp hot water
>
>1½ tsp ground annatto (achiote)

Place in refrigerator to cool.

Cut into small pieces

>5 Tbsp cold butter

Return to refrigerator to keep cold.

Combine and mix well

> 1½ cups flour
> 2 Tbsp sugar
> ½ tsp baking powder
> ½ tsp baking soda
> ⅛ tsp salt

When the annatto water is cool prepare the dough. The end result you want is like pie crust, properly prepared the empanadas will be light and flaky – over mixing will cause them to be heavy and tough. Add and cut in with a butter knife, until the largest pieces are about the size of a pea – do not stir, beat or attempt to achieve a smooth texture.

> Butter pieces

Combine

> Annatto water
> 1 lightly beaten egg
> ½ tsp vanilla

Stir this into the flour mixture, 1 Tbsp at a time, mixing as little as possible - the end result should still be somewhat floury. Gather the mixture into a ball – sort of kneading – but just enough to hold together and not be floury. Wrap in plastic wrap and refrigerate at least 30 minutes.

In a small saucepan, bring to simmer for 10 minutes, stirring frequently to avoid scorching and boilovers

> 1½ cups milk
> Zest from ½ orange
> ¼ tsp cinnamon

Lightly beat together

> 1 egg yolk
> 2 Tbsp sugar
> 1¾ Tbsp cornstarch
> ¼ tsp vanilla extract
> ⅛ tsp salt

Add 1 Tbsp of hot milk into the egg mixture, stirring constantly. Repeat with another Tbsp milk. Add the egg mixture to the remaining milk and whisk over low heat constantly until the mixture begins to thicken, about 2 minutes. Allow mixture to cool to room temperature for 30 minutes before using.

Both the dough and the custard can be made well in advance.

Preheat oven to 350°F. Remove the dough from the refrigerator and, on a well-floured surface, roll until ⅛-inch thick. Using a 3-inch biscuit or cookie cutter, cut out circles from dough. Collect dough scraps, reroll, and repeat until all the dough is used. You should have about 24 circles.

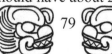

79

Fill each circle with about 1 Tbsp cooled filling. Carefully fold the dough in half, taking care to keep the filling inside the pocket. Press the edges shut and then seal using the tines of a fork.

Place the empanadas on cookie sheets and bake for 15 to 20 minutes, taking care not to let them burn. Ideally serve warm.

## Evaporated Milk Custard – Flan de Leche Condensada

A quickie version of flan.

Preheat oven to 350° and heat a large pan with about 1″ water – a Bain Marie

Combine well in a blender or with a mixer

    1 14oz can sweetened condensed milk (Eagle brand)

    1 14oz can water

    6 eggs

    1 tsp vanilla

Place the mixture in a soufflé dish or several ramekins. Place in the Bain Marie and bake for 25-30 minutes until a sharp knife inserted comes out clean. Refrigerate until cold.

## Milk Caramel Sauce – Dulce de Leche

Often used as a topping for ice cream or sweet breads such as muffins. Very traditional, but time consuming to make.

In a large heavy saucepan over medium heat, scald

    2 qt milk

Reduce heat to low and continue to cook, stirring frequently to avoid boil-overs and prevent the bottom from scorching. After half an hour add

    1 cup packed brown sugar

    2 tsp cinnamon

Continue stirring frequently. When reduced to about 1½ cups – about an hour and a half later, add

    3 lightly beaten eggs

Continue stirring frequently for about half an hour.

## Plantains with Mole Sauce – Mole de Plátano

This recipe calls for chocolate with cinnamon. In a well stocked supermarket with a Latin American section or in a Latin American grocery you can probably find "Chocolate". It is lightly sweetened and a bit grainier than western chocolate and is primarily used for making "moles" or hot chocolate beverage. It is most often plain, but is sometimes seasoned with cinnamon (canela) or vanilla (vainilla).

If the version without cinnamon is available, add to the recipe

    ¼ tsp cinnamon

If "chocolate" is not available, combine
      1oz unsweetened baking chocolate
      1 tsp sugar
      ¼ tsp cinnamon
Toast
      2 slices bread
Peel and cut into ⅜"- ½" slices
      4 ripe plantains – a ripe plantain is black or nearly black
In a large skillet over medium heat
      2 Tbsp oil
Fry the plantain slices until lightly browned on each side
Toast in a skillet (preferably cast iron, to avoid warping or delamination of the pan)
      ½ cup dried pumpkin seeds
      2 Tbsp sesame seeds
      6 whole cloves
Coarsely chop
      8-10 Roma tomatoes
Cook for about 10 minutes with
      1 chile ancho (pasa) with seeds and stem removed
In a blender, purée
      Toasted bread, broken into pieces
      1oz roughly chopped chocolate as described above
      ¼ tsp cinnamon
      Toasted seeds and cloves
      ½ tsp ground achiote
      Tomatoes and chili
      ¾ cup sugar
      1 tsp salt
Place in a large skillet or saucepan and bring to a boil. Add the fried plantains and serve.

## Plantain and Cannellini Bean Pancakes – Panqueques de Plátano y Frijoles Blancos

Excellent as a breakfast dish or as a dessert
In a food processor, pulse until well mixed, leaving some texture
      1 cup drained canned cannellini beans
      1 very ripe plantain

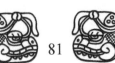

In a large bowl, mix until combined

> Beans and plantain
> ½ tsp ground cinnamon
> 2 Tbsp honey
> 1 large lightly beaten egg
> 3 Tbsp flour

Preheat oven to 200°F

Lightly oil a nonstick skillet and heat on medium high. Drop quarter cups of the mixture onto the hot skillet – as many as possible without touching one another. Cook 3-4 minutes per side, until golden brown. Place in warm oven while cooking the remaining batter – you may need to lightly oil the skillet between batches. Serve warm with butter and honey.

## Sweet Stuffed Chayotes – Chancletas de Guisquil

Steam until fork tender

> 4 chayotes (güisquiles)

After cooling a bit, cut in half lengthwise, remove the seed and scoop out most of the flesh, leaving the shells (skins) intact.

Add to the güisquil flesh and mix well

> 1 tsp cinnamon
> ¼ cup heavy cream
> ¼ cup raisins
> ¾ cup breadcrumbs
> 1 tsp sugar
> 1 Tbsp melted butter

Preheat oven to 350°

Fill the güisquil shells with the pulp mixture in place on a baking sheet. Bake in preheated oven for 10-15 minutes.

# Notes

# Notes

# Notes

# Notes

# Notes

Made in the USA
Las Vegas, NV
03 March 2022

44899281R00057